Body Language

by Rebecca Weber

Content Adviser: David B. Givens, Ph.D., Director,
Center for Nonverbal Studies, Spokane, Washington

Reading Adviser: Rosemary G. Palmer, Ph.D.,
Department of Literacy, College of Education,
Boise State University

Spyglass
BOOKS

COMPASS POINT BOOKS

Minneapolis, Minnesota

Compass Point Books
3109 West 50th Street, #115
Minneapolis, MN 55410

Visit Compass Point Books on the Internet at *www.compasspointbooks.com*
or e-mail your request to *custserv@compasspointbooks.com*

Photographs ©: Gary Sundermeyer, cover; PhotoDisc, 4, 5, 13, 14, 16; Ariel Skelley/Corbis, 6; Michael S. Yamashita/Corbis, 7; Ronnen Eshel/Corbis, 8; Brand X Pictures, 9, 11; Jose Luis Pelaez, Inc./Corbis, 10; Stockbyte, 12, 17; Rubberball Productions, 15; Rolf Bruderer/Corbis, 18; E. O. Hoppé/Corbis, 19.

Creative Director: Terri Foley
Managing Editor: Catherine Neitge
Editor: Jennifer VanVoorst
Photo Researcher: Svetlana Zhurkina
Designer: Les Tranby
Educational Consultant: Diane Smolinski

Library of Congress Cataloging-in-Publication Data
Weber, Rebecca.
   Body language / by Rebecca Weber.
     v. cm. — (Spyglass books)
Includes bibliographical references and index.
Contents: Body talk—Nice to meet you—Listening to each other—Happy or not—Different meanings—What do your hands say?
   ISBN 0-7565-0650-6 (hardcover)
   1. Body language—Juvenile literature. [1. Body language.] I. Title. II. Series.
BF637.N66W435 2004
153.6'9—dc22   2003024096

Contents

NOTE: Glossary words are in **bold** the first time they appear.

Body Talk

Have you ever watched two people talk to each other?

They might say one thing with words. They might say something different, though, with their bodies.

Body language can often tell you what people are thinking and feeling.

Nice to Meet You

Watch to see how two people greet each other.

If they lean forward and smile, they are happy to meet. If they lean sideways, they are nervous or uneasy.

Many Asian people bow to each other when they say hello. People in Japan bow more deeply when they meet someone they respect.

American adults often shake hands to greet one another. If they use both hands to shake, they like each other a lot.

Squeezing too hard while shaking hands shows that people do not like each other very much.

Sometimes people hug
or even kiss each other
to say hello.

Listening to Each Other

Watch to see how two people listen to one another.

People who really listen might tilt their head to one side. They might look into the eyes of the person who is speaking.

Sometimes people who are listening nod their heads. Sometimes nodding means they agree or understand. Other times nodding means they just want to talk.

Body language can also show when people are not listening.

People who are *slumped* over, *staring* into space, or tapping their feet may not really be listening.

Doodling can be a sign of boredom. People who are bored are probably not listening very closely.

13

Happy or Not

Body language can show
when a person is happy.

When people are happy, they do
not just smile with their mouths.
Their eyes will crinkle, too.

Look into a person's eyes. Are the *pupils* large? Large pupils could mean this person likes what he or she sees!

Body language can also show
when a person is angry or unhappy.

People who lean forward with
their hands on their hips are not
happy. If their hands are curled
into fists, they may be angry.

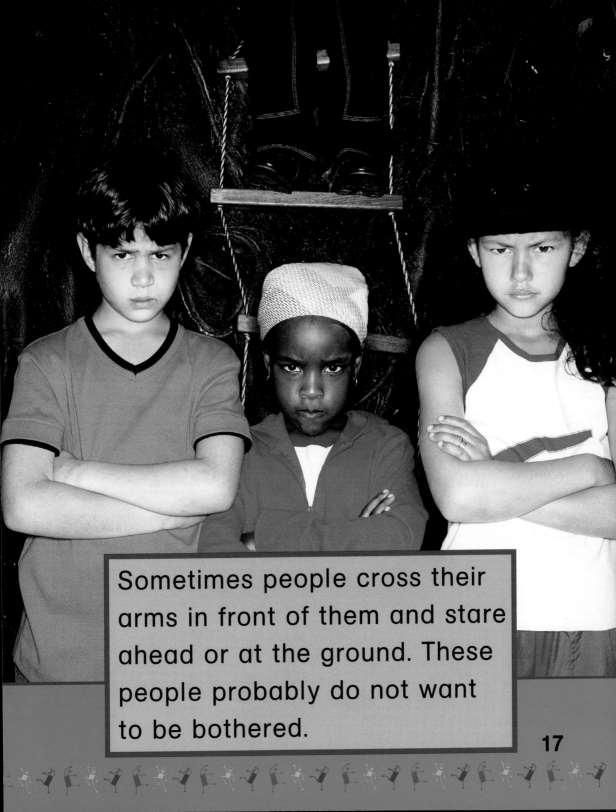

Sometimes people cross their arms in front of them and stare ahead or at the ground. These people probably do not want to be bothered.

Different Meanings

People from different countries use different body language.

Americans wave hello or good-bye with their hands. In Europe, this same wave can mean "no" or "stop."

The native people of New
Zealand touch their noses
and foreheads together
when they meet.

19

What Do Your Hands Say?

Americans sometimes use these hand signs to speak with their hands.

A. Everything is OK.

B. I am angry!

C. Peace

D. Stop

E. Good

F. Bad

G. Hi! *or* Good-bye!

H. Over there

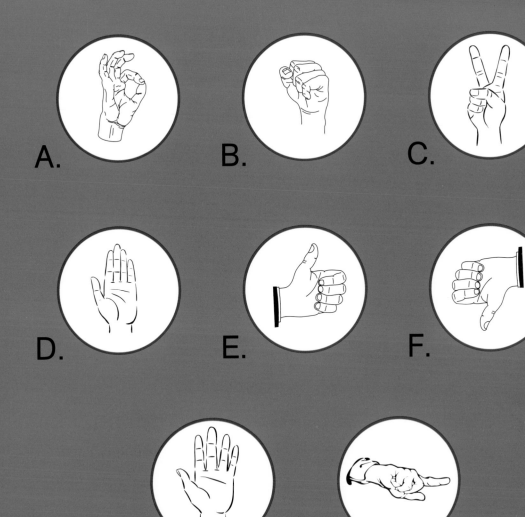

A.

B.

C.

D.

E.

F.

G.

H.

Glossary

body language–the way a person moves his or her body or behaves around another person or other people

doodling–drawing or writing without paying attention

pupils–the black circles in the middle of a person's eyeballs

slumped–with sagging shoulders

staring–looking at something for a long time without moving your eyes

Learn More

Books

Price Hossell, Karen. *Body Language.*
    Chicago: Heinemann Library, 2002.
Robson, Pam. *Body Language.* New York:
    Franklin Watts, 1997.

On the Web

For more information on *Body Language,*
use FactHound to track down Web sites
related to this book.

1. Go to *www.facthound.com*
2. Type in a search word related
   to this book or this book ID:
   0756506506.
3. Click on the *Fetch It* button.

Your trusty FactHound will fetch
the best Web sites for you!

Index

GR: I
Word Count: 241

From Rebecca Weber

Whenever I travel to a new place, I enjoy learning about people and their daily lives. I hope this book opens up a little bit of the world for you!